Faithful French Bulldogs

A COLOURING BOOK FOR ADULTS

Paws for Thought: Vol. 5

Christine Vencato

This book is dedicated to my wonderful family

Illustrations and design © 2016 Christine Vencato

www.arttherapycolouringbook.org

First edition; first printing

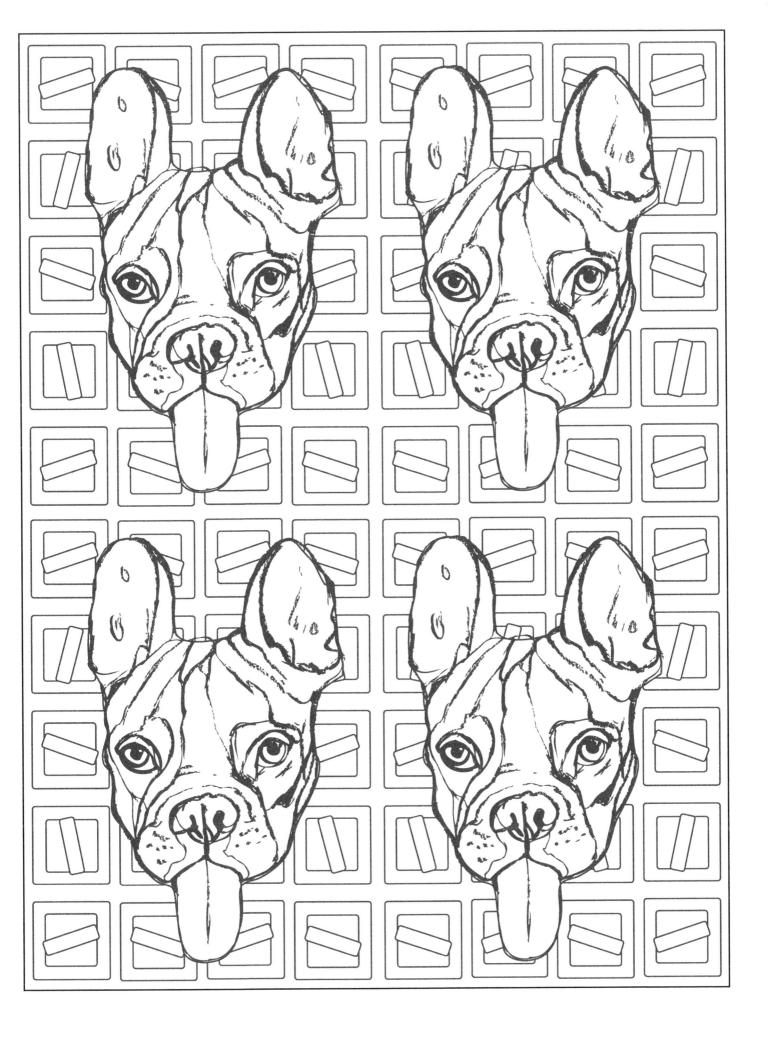

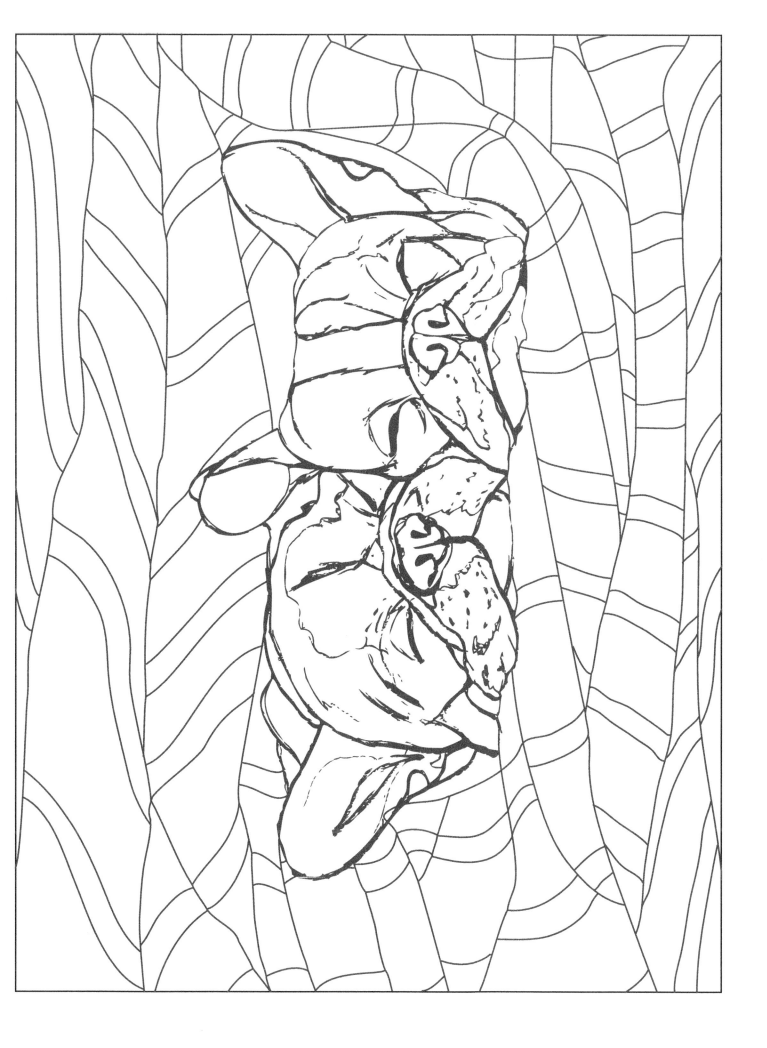

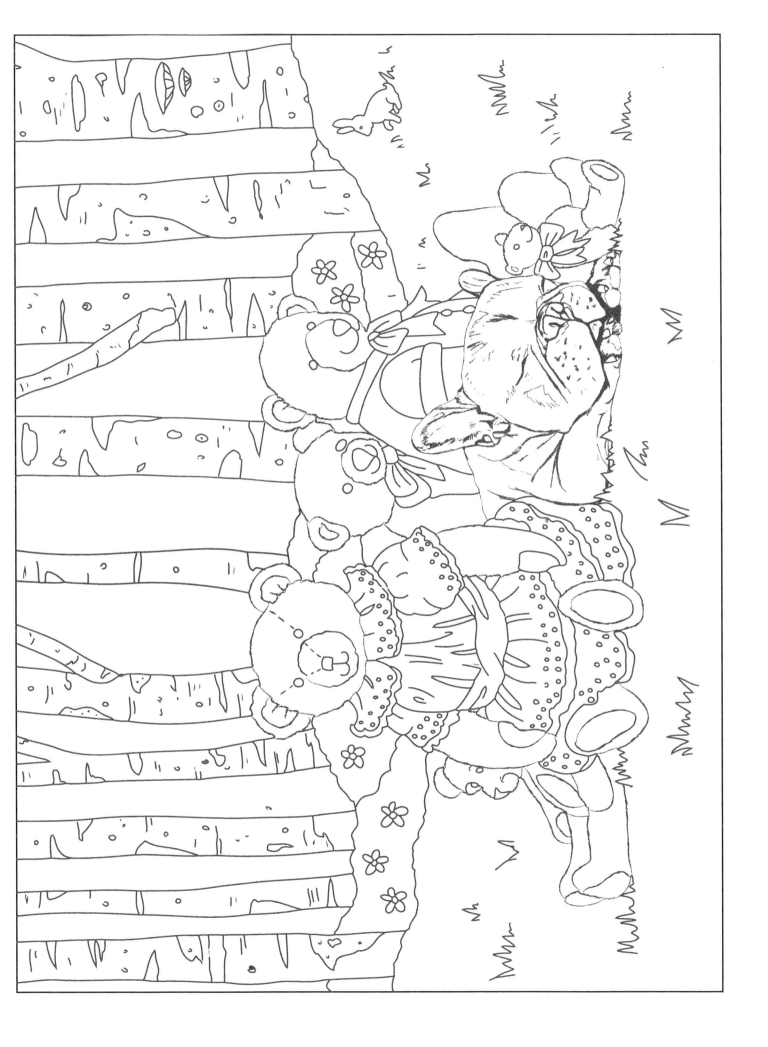

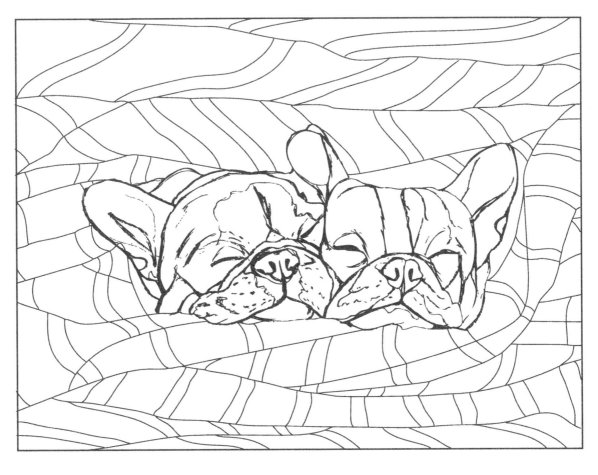

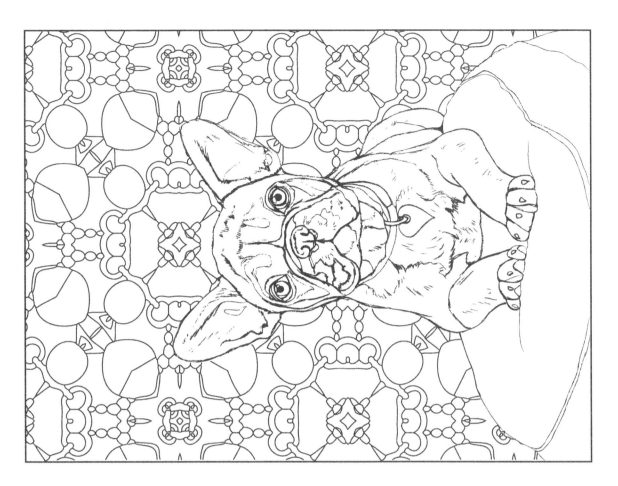

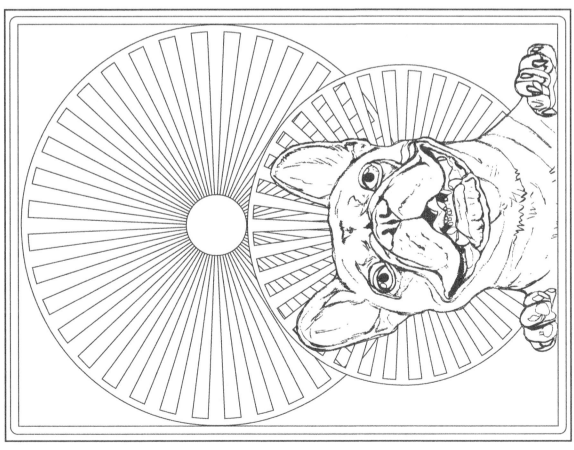

PLEASE VISIT WWW.ARTTHERAPYCOLOURINGBOOK.ORG FOR MORE INFORMATION AND FREE COLOURING PAGES. YOU MAY ALSO BE INTERESTED IN OTHER BOOKS FROM THE SAME AUTHOR:

Darling Dachshunds
A COLOURING BOOK FOR ADULTS
Paws for Thought: Vol. 1
Christine Vencato

Precious Pugs
A COLOURING BOOK FOR ADULTS
Paws for Thought: Vol. 2
Christine Vencato

Lovely Labrador & Golden Retrievers
A COLOURING BOOK FOR ADULTS
Paws for Thought: Vol. 3
Christine Vencato

Gentle German Shepherds
A COLOURING BOOK FOR ADULTS
Paws for Thought: Vol. 4
Christine Vencato

Made in the USA
Monee, IL
13 December 2019